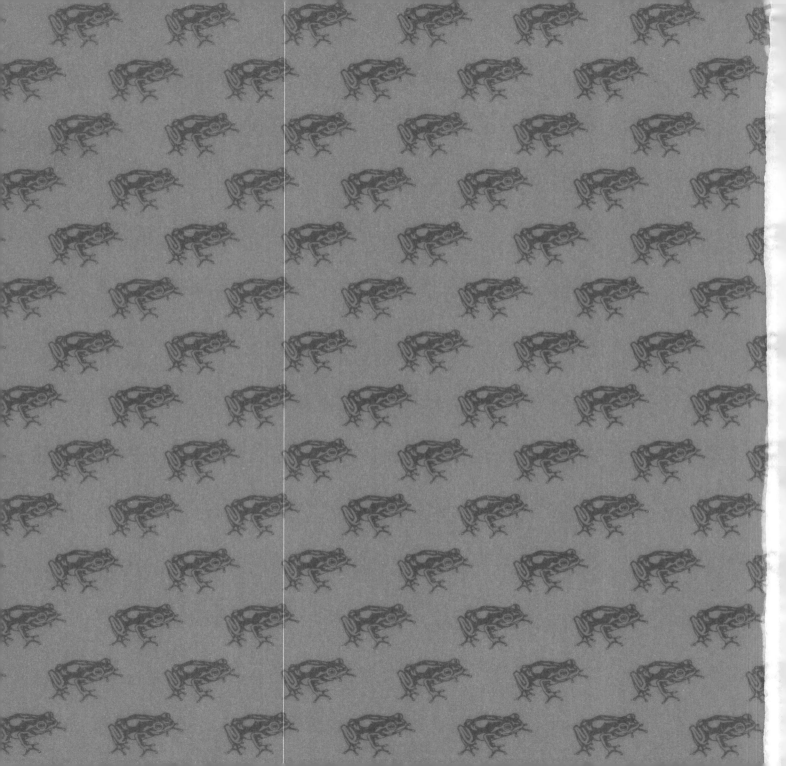

frog

CUTTING EDGE

FAY SWEET

frog

Form Follows Emotion

THAMES AND HUDSON

First published in Great Britain
in 1999 by Thames and Hudson Ltd, London

Design copyright © 1999 The Ivy Press

Text copyright © 1999 The Ivy Press

British Library Cataloguing-in-Publication Data

A catalogue record for this book is
available from the British Library

ISBN 0-500-01917-7

Originated and printed by Hong Kong Graphic,
Hong Kong

Contents

'Frog stands for the best in creative design services. We are a new kind of world-class business: a global creative network that generates substantial return on investment for our clients in every sense of the term. Our charter is to evolve with courage, grace, and a pure heart, to always focus on being the leader, and to embrace new forms of creative collaboration. We achieve this by embodying a magic mixture of characteristics that include being radical, inspirational and optimistic; fun, flexible and young of mind. But most important we are ethical, tolerant, caring and hardworking. Then, "form follows emotion".'

Hartmut Esslinger

'We believe consumers don't just buy a product, they buy value in the form of entertainment, experience and self-identity.'

AS ANY CHILD WILL TELL YOU, in fairy tales the frog is always miraculously transformed into a handsome prince. A kiss from a beautiful princess is all it takes to unlock inner beauty and turn the toady ugliness into Hollywood good looks – and everyone lives happily ever after. Now, in real life, a frog has turned the tables. The frog in this case is one of the world's most successful strategic design companies; it has within its power the ability to sprinkle magic and secure the fortunes of any number of corporations. This company has put many others on the map, helping redraw the territory in countless sectors from home entertainment and computers to dentistry and clinical research. Its client list ranges from university student start-ups to blue chip multinationals including Apple Computer, Louis Vuitton, Olympus, NEC, Kodak, Motorola, Packard Bell, Sony, Logitech, AT&T and Lufthansa.

The success of many of the projects is unequivocal; the designs are must-haves, they look great, feel great, they work, and they often reach classic status within months of their launch. The Sony Trinitron redefined television design; the Olympus BX-40 microscope has been lauded as industrial sculpture and is now the world's best-selling clinical microscope; the colourful Hansgrohe showerhead for Tribel is to be found in bathrooms all over Europe – it pioneered the idea of washing as a lifestyle experience and has sold more than 15 million units to date.

The sleek flat-screen Sony Trinitron, launched in 1978, heralded a breakthrough at a time when other TVs were cased in wood-effect boxes.

Simple yet smart: frog's upright answering machine for AT&T was America's best-seller for five years.

8

Time and again the kiss of the frog has made companies leap to life. When Apple wanted to launch the Macintosh computer it called in frog to complete the design; revenue soared from $700 million in 1982 to $4 billion in 1986. Likewise work on the corporate logo, pointing devices and packaging for Logitech saw revenue climb steeply from $43 million in 1988 to over $200 million in 1995, securing the company its number one market position. Number crunchers have worked out that frog-designed products rack up sales of $30 billion per annum.

The extra dimension

The alchemy performed by frog is based on a formula devised by the company's founder Hartmut Esslinger: Form Follows Emotion. He believes product design should always include something extra: 'The magic is when both the manufacturer and consumer get something good that they don't expect.' For Esslinger, no matter how elegant and functional a design, it will not win a place in our lives unless it can appeal at a deeper level, to our emotions. 'We believe consumers don't just buy a product, they buy value in the form of entertainment, experience and self-identity.' The emotional element can be present in any number of ways: it may appeal to our desire for enhanced nostalgia, as in the designs for Dual electronics, or it might be a tactile ergonomic experience, as deployed in a computer games joystick that is sculpted to fit snugly in the hand. Or it could be in reinventing the familiar: the massive-selling AT&T answering machine was flipped on its side, with the dual emotional pay-offs of showing consumer individuality and helping to keep a desk tidy.

Now in his mid-50s, tall and slim with a mop of dark curls and wearing jeans and T-shirt, Hartmut Esslinger looks as though he might be in the music business. He certainly plays a mean jazz piano and has a stunning ebony Bösendorfer grand in his office. But design is Esslinger's passion. 'I might have gone into music, but there were plenty of others who were better than me,' he declares. 'In any case, I really only wanted to design. I wanted to make people happy, that's what I came into this world for.'

Esslinger has been aware of the power of good, intriguing design right from his childhood — his parents worked in fashion and ran a clothes store. 'Even as a kid I was good at forecasting what people would like,' he says. After a short time in the army Esslinger went to college, but soon moved from engineering to the design course. 'They were all obsessed with clean lines, the machine aesthetic; they wanted to strip objects back to their basic function and make them emotion-free. It was so dull, I hated it.' Although Esslinger admired German designers such as Dieter Rams ('He turned functional design into art'), his heroes were Italians such as the Castiglione brothers, Ettore Sottsass, Enzo Mari and Joe Colombo, all producing exuberant, exciting work.

Toast Logic's friendly styling and ingenious viewing window mark this toaster out from the crowd.

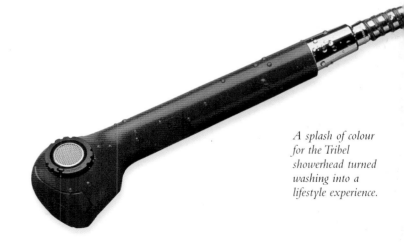

A splash of colour for the Tribel showerhead turned washing into a lifestyle experience.

9

'When I was starting up in business it was the late 1960s, a time of change,' Esslinger recalls. 'Man had landed on the moon, young people wanted to change the world, we all wanted to make a difference. I wanted to make people smile. If you can make people smile and get them excited they enjoy life better. A person driving a Porsche has a different feeling from someone driving a sheet metal box. If you build in emotional value, people will keep the product longer and take more care of it; this of course also saves energy and materials. It's the difference between selling an ordinary hi-fi and selling amazing sound.'

From a tadpole

Just like a fairy tale, Esslinger started his company in a small shed at his home in Altensteig in the German Black Forest. As business grew so did the offices, and today frog's base is in the post-modern strip of Sunnyvale in California's Silicon Valley. Inside the pastel-coloured building, the interior has been gutted, deconstructed and rebuilt with huge inclining walls clad with recycled newspaper board. Concrete beams are exposed and silver air conditioning shafts hang from the underbelly of the ceiling. It's raw and vital. The hum of activity is only broken at 4pm when everyone stops work for coffee and cakes.

Thirty years on there's still an office in Altensteig, but the frog pond has grown to include others in Düsseldorf (opening spring 1999), San Francisco, New York and Austin, Texas. Each office has its own character and specialisms. Austin and San Francisco, for example, specialize in new media and digital user-interface design, working on projects such as the world's most responsive remote control handsets. The New York office, established in 1998, is slightly different. Here frog offers the full range of design skills, from graphics and product to digital work. It is headed by Tucker Viemeister, formerly of the respected product design outfit Smart Design. 'I think of myself as multi-dimensional or post-disciplinary designer, and my dream is to build a team to work like that here,' says Viemeister. 'I want industrial designers working on Web sites, graphic designers creating 3-D shapes, engineers doing graphics. This mix of input happens at the start, then as the project progresses individuals can switch back to their areas of expertise.' The goal of building the dream team is shared with Esslinger, who has always encouraged the contributions of everyone working on a project – engineers have their say on design, and designers pitch in on materials and systems. No single person is credited; each project is the product of team work.

Early in his career Esslinger's big break came with a commission from the German electronics giant Wega. He was spotted after winning a student competition and was invited to design a new television. It was a big hit. It was the first of more than 100 products he designed for the company. A few years later Wega was

Ergonomics meets elegance in this computer games joystick for Techmedia.

'If you build in emotional value, people will keep the product longer and take more care of it.'

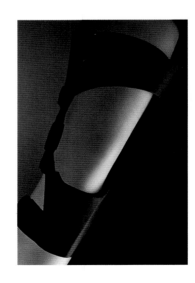

The flexible joint of this frog-designed kneebrace imitates the complex movement of the human knee.

bought by Sony, and Esslinger soon found himself working for this massive corporation – his first success was the mould-breaking black-box Sony Trinitron TV. Gradually Esslinger Design and then frogdesign (as the company was named in 1982; the name changed to frog in 1998) became synonymous with innovation, risk-taking, vision and success.

It was precisely this mix that appealed to top executive Steve Jobs when he was searching for the elusive magic that would give his computer company Apple a market edge. The year was 1981 and computing was a sea of anonymous beige boxes. Jobs combed the world for a strategy-focused design company, and knew he'd found it in frog. So sure was he that a multi-million dollar deal was struck which enticed Esslinger to establish a Californian office. The product of this relationship was the Mac SE, with its chic, user-friendly hardware. With a foothold in Silicon Valley and proof with every job that design can be a competitive weapon, frog's list of high-profile clients grew and grew.

The memorable company name must have helped in frog's ascendancy. Esslinger throws some light on its provenance: 'There are various theories about where the name came from. It's actually the nickname given to people from my home town. Altensteig is on the migrating route of millions of frogs – at certain times of the year they even shut the highways to let the frogs pass. The name appealed to me. Everyone thought it was a little stupid, but I was stubborn and insisted. Of course now it has different connotations: it's green and capable of making great leaps, but is also unpredictable. I suppose if Altensteig had been known for its cows or its sheep it would have been a very different story.'

The business of design

Esslinger has never faltered in his belief that design is more than putting together appealing shapes and colours – the emotional content is crucial to a product's success and therefore to its business performance. And he makes no pretence at playing the artist disinterested in real-life concerns – for him, a product does not succeed unless it sells. It is this welding of design skills with business understanding that has appealed to so many corporate sales managers and CEOs and earned Esslinger a prestigious place on the cover of US news magazine *BusinessWeek*. He is the only living designer to have been given this honour since the design giant Raymond Loewy was featured there in 1934. Inside, Esslinger was described as 'the most influential industrial designer on the American scene since the 1930s'.

An early Esslinger design: the Wega 3072 colour stereo TV.

Frog's stamped metal door for Amdahl mainframe computers combines aesthetic appeal with improved structural strength.

Although crucially aware of his clients' business needs, Esslinger has seen frog's own fortunes take a rollercoaster ride. There have been times when the studio mix has been out of tune, and staff turnover has been rapid. Considered by many to be a genius, Esslinger is also a demanding and sometimes volatile boss. He has been capable of massive distractions too: frox, his late 1980s venture to create and produce one of the first multimedia home entertainment centres, ended in failure with losses of $2 million. The investment of so much time, money and energy left frog considerably weakened. But today frog is back on dry land; it has undergone its own redesign and looks stronger and more focused than ever before.

Although he retains a strong German accent, Esslinger has embraced America wholeheartedly. 'Europe is like my mom – I love her but I don't want to live with her any more. The US offers freedom, and it's a very practical and pragmatic place. Everything is negotiated, everyone has their say, then they make a deal and it has to work. Even environmental issues are treated that way – politicians want to get elected, people want clean air, and so the politicians must find a way to clean up. It's horrifying to European intellectuals, but it works and I find it liberating.' Similar bald logic applies to design projects: 'People want products that work, look good and don't damage the environment, and businesses want to make profits. They pay us to find the solution.'

The one-stop shop

And along with his philosophy of form following emotion, Esslinger is convinced that frog's newly evolved holistic approach – called Integrated Strategic Design and Communications – must be the way forward. 'Aesthetics are only part of our job; the integrated process allows us to look at products, brands or companies as a whole,' he says. 'We can take a project from the idea stage right through to the sale – and that might include product design, engineering, production, graphics, logos, packaging and digital media. There's no point spending a fortune on graphic design if the product doesn't work.' With some clients this means reappraising their whole approach. 'With Lufthansa we looked at their entire operation from ticket sales to destination. We improved the check-in counters, redesigned the airport signage and upgraded the lounges to make them more comfortable and romantic, reminiscent of the elegant days of flying. We also redesigned the plane interiors, the seats, the cutlery... It's the whole package of design, communication, delivery. When one element is wrong it can spoil the whole, and these days no one can afford to let that happen.'

To make this integrated, one-stop shop approach work, frog employs staff from a cross-section of disciplines from model makers, paint specialists and engineers to software writers, behavioural psychologists and 3-D designers. There are experts in three key areas: brand and strategy, product development, and new media.

Every frog-designed logo has instant impact and layers of meaning.

Packard Bell

LUNARIS

The Mac of the Future? Frog deconstructed the Apple Macintosh into a series of sculptural elements for a 1996 prototype design commissioned by Macworld magazine.

The product design process follows a prescribed route of investigation, exploration, definition, implementation, preparation and production. 'For each project, a specialized, multi-disciplinary team is assembled – no job is ever attributed to a single designer, they are all the result of team work,' explains president of product development Dan Harden. 'We start with a closed-door brainstorming "jam session" to discover the conceptual essence. Some ideas will be straightforward, some will be completely crazy. We're not afraid to be risky because innovation is risky, and we're also not afraid to follow our intuition. Market research is very useful up to a point, but we often transcend this by seeking the hidden dimension of "consumer need", so that the user is ultimately surprised and delighted.'

Harden describes the design process: 'We get into 3-D models and CAD [computer-aided design] right away. This rapid visualization is critical, because speed-to-market is often the first client objective. Concurrent and holistic problem-solving on every level, simultaneously, is the challenge.' He cites the revolutionary ice hockey skate designed for Würthner as an example. 'It was outrageous to think up a skate which could support a 300lb hockey player, travelling at great speed, on a 0.4mm strip of tungsten steel. But we took the risk to go down that road, called in the help of materials experts, and did it. We made a skate that was lighter and faster than any other.' In this process of 'creative orchestration', says Harden, 'industrial design issues like usability and form must harmonize with engineering issues such as manufacturability, performance and cost.'

When these different elements gel, it makes a powerful mix. 'Something magical happens – the customer resonates with the product on an emotional level, which can be the beginning of a deep brand loyalty.' This area is the responsibility of frog's brand strategist, Gregory Hom. 'Developing a retail brand involves understanding the millions of details in its make up,' he says. 'It's not just a label, it's the representations of everything to do with a product, the look of the graphics, the attitude of the staff, the way the phone is answered, the smell of the coffee, all the details that set up an expectation. Not only does everything matter, but everything is connected to everything else.' And as business becomes increasingly aware of brand values, the importance of an integrated approach in design becomes ever more important. 'For maximum inpact there must be congruity between the two-dimensional aspects, such as graphics, the 3-D products, and then the digital story – the Web sites and e-commerce', says Hom, Frog's brand team members are charged with ensuring that the message is consistent.

To complement the brand and strategy work and the product design work, frog's third key area of expertise is new media. Here the skills of frog's graphic designers are combined with those of

Taking a holistic approach to Lufthansa's image, frog's work for the company has included everything from check-in counters to airline seats.

'Europe is like my mom – I love her but I don't want to live with her any more. The US offers freedom, and it's a very practical and pragmatic place.'

13

software experts. The image is always compelling and invites you to explore. 'Our interest is in interaction,' says new media president Doreen Lorenzo. 'We work on intuitive ways for people to use products. It might be a television remote control or the panel on the front of a music system, but whatever the user interface it should be clear and logical.' In addition there is the production of CD-ROMs and Web design work. 'Good Web design is all about assessing how the user is going to interact. For example if we are working on a computer company's Web site we want to make sure the site visitor gets from it what they want – if they are a business user and they want to make a purchase then they must be directed straight to the sales pages; if they are a private buyer looking for information they must be able to make their way to it quickly. New media has the potential to distinguish brands – if one phone is easier to programme than another then that makes all the difference to the user.'

The fairy tale has come true, Esslinger and his teams have consistently transformed ideas into reality and continue to make strategic design an integral part of commercial success. With every new project, the frog story continues in leaps and bounds.

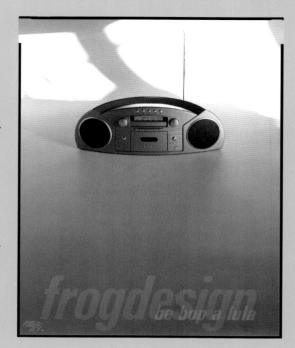

'Aesthetics are only part of our job; the integrated process allows us to look at products, brands or companies as a whole.'

Hartmut Esslinger believes that if you're proud of your work, then you should shout about it. Ever since the mid-1970s frog's projects have featured on the back pages of the world's leading design magazines, including Form *and* ID. *The eye-catching and high-profile ads have won admiration from fellow designers and have helped attract important clients.*

frogdesign
the power of beauty

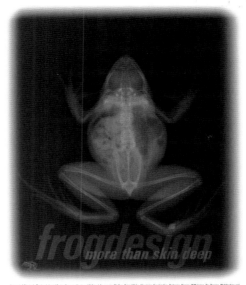

frogdesign
more than skin deep

Integrated Strategic Design: Industrial Design, Corporate Identity and Collateral, Engineering, MacCom, Point of Sales, Advertising, User Interface, Packaging, Naming, OEM Liaison, Dry Cleaning, Multimaking and Packaging, the creation of the complete brand and product experience involving hardware, software and wetware. **frogdesign California/USA**, 1327 Chesapeake Terrace, Sunnyvale, CA 94089. Tel: (1) 408 734 5800, Fax: (1) 408 734 5805. E-mail: info@frogsf.com. **frogdesign Germany**, Germany, 33, D-72213 Altensteig, Tel: (49) 07453 2740, Fax: (49) 07453 2 9636. All ideas, concepts and designs created by the members of the frogdesign studios or associated members are the result of an interactive team process.

frogdesign
how the web was won

ISDC - Integrated Strategic Design & Communications: Web Development.
frogdesign Studios in Silicon Valley, Tel: (1) 408 734 5800; San Francisco, Tel: (1) 415 442 4804; Austin, Tel: (1) 512 477 3764;
New York, Tel: (1) 212 965 9700; Altensteig, Tel: (49) 07453 2740. E-mail: info@frogdesign.com or info@frogdesign.com www.frogdesign.com
All ideas, concepts and designs created by the members of the frogdesign studios or associated members are the result of an interactive team process.

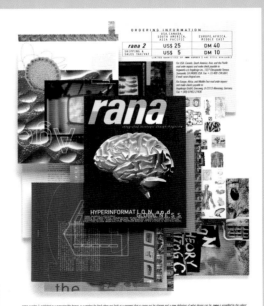

rana number 2: published in a magazine-like format, is a catalyst for fresh ideas set forth in a moment that is crying out for change and a new definition of what design can be. **rana** is propelled by the salient fact that both the media and our competitors have opted for convenient nostalgia precisely at the moment when a richer, more strategic vision of the globe is needed. We want **rana** to be a credible and ethical statement in increasingly manipulative and post-credible times.

15

FROG LOGOS
Corporate logos, 1982
and 1998

**Friedolin, Hartmut Esslinger's
pet Brazilian tree frog,
provided the model for the
company's first logo. With the
1998 name change and focus
on an integrated strategic
approach to design came
semi-retirement for Friedolin
and the new 'serious fun' logo
in bold colours.**

IT WOULD BE A TOUGH challenge to find a
design company with a logo more instantly
recognizable than frog's. Right from the start
of his career, Esslinger held a firm belief in the
need for designers to promote themselves and
their work, wanting to demonstrate that design
wasn't just an add-on but part of a company's
marketing armoury. Thus the line drawing of
Hartmut Esslinger's pet Brazilian tree frog,
Friedolin, achieved global fame through its
appearances in the regular back page ads that
over the past 20 years have appeared in the
world's most important design magazines.

But to mark a new phase in its operations –
the opening of offices in New York, San Francisco and Düsseldorf, and its ability to offer a
fully integrated, strategic consultancy – frog in
the summer of 1998 unveiled a new corporate
identity. Friedolin has leapt off the page to be
replaced by just the word 'frog'. The word is
always shown with lower case letters, each in a
bright nursery school colour – it is youthful, but
there is also underlying restraint and formality.
As Esslinger explains: 'The new brand is about
serious fun; it symbolizes a company that is
dynamic, diverse, culturally rich and full of passion. The colour green is a reminder of frog's
amphibious heritage, and the remaining three
colours represent the bright palette of talent we
can draw on.' The disappearance of Friedolin is
typical of frog – avoid the predictable, and keep
everyone guessing. But the much-loved
amphibian has not gone forever. 'Friedolin will
be allowed to play a new and mysterious role
within the corporate identity system,' says creative director Gregory Hom.

**Providing a platform for
experimental imagery and
wide-ranging debate, frog's
provocative magazine *rana*
aims at challenging
preconceptions in the design
world and beyond.**

design must
transcend
needs, wants,
and even
dreams – it
must harness
a vision.

hartmut esslinger, president, and steven skov holt, director, strategic design

Can design change the world?
Yes, we believe it can. For the
G7 nations (France, Germany,
Great Britain, Italy, Japan,
Spain, and the United States),
the 1950s were the Age of
Production, the 1960s were the
Age of R&D, the 1970s were
the Age of Marketing, and the 1980s were the Age of Finance. The 1990s
are the time to take all that we have learned and put it together. It is a moment
of integration. The 1990s are the Age of Integrated Strategic Design (ISD).
Our time is different in other ways as well. For the first time in the history of mankind, we can build
silicon-based tools for any task we want. Ours is a moment when we have too
much technology and not enough thought. A moment when we have too much
brainless junk, and not enough junkless brains. A moment when change is the
biggest story in the world today, but no one covers it. A moment when the
proportion between a person and the nearly infinite space of our galaxy is
about the same as the proportion between a person and the nearly infinite
smallness of our tiniest particles. A moment when there is more information
to process than we ever have time to turn into wisdom. A moment when sports
teams, computer companies and rock bands inspire more loyalty than
religions. A moment when replicas are often favored over the real thing. A
moment, in short, of unbelievable opportunities.
At frogdesign, We Have Certain Beliefs
We believe the focus of our profession must become "People in Harmony
with Nature and Industry." We must make this a production value expected
by consumer, retailer and manufacturer alike. For us, it is a matter of small
steps and persistent improvement, as much as order-of-magnitude differences
and paradigm shifts.

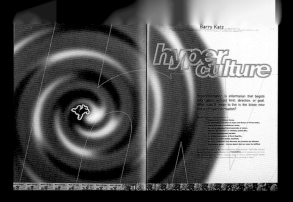

RANA
Spreads, issue 2, 1996

The second issue of frog's 'integrated strategic design magazine' focused on the topic of 'hyperinformation and globalness'. Thought-provoking articles dealt with issues such as digital user interfaces, information overload and the concept of 'post-industrial' design.

Visual Overload

Cyberpunk fiction describes information as a great teeming city — a "sprawl" (William Gibson) or "metaverse" (Neal Stephenson) of files and figures. The visually busy city, from Picadilly to Times Square to the Ginza, is not new. Indeed, modern art prefigures the collage-like atmosphere of the post-modern city.

In *High and Low*, the catalog for the New York Museum of Modern Art's exhibition of several years ago, curators Adam Gopnick and Kirk Varnedoe argue that the devices of early Cubism, including the use of torn newspaper **fragments**, were a response to the visual overload of Paris in the first years of this century. Gopnick and Varnedoe argue that an information explosion had surrounded the artists with newsstands, kiosks, billboards and posters through which images, words, colors, textures, and letters became powerfully juxtaposed in context and scale.

The works of Pablo Picasso and Georges Braque suggest a response to overload — that it can be not just defensive but creative. By "editing and recombining the world of print," as the curators put it, they made a new and highly personal reality within the overload — this creative misinterpretation was *defensive*, but it was also triumphant — an order, again, of association rather than of categorization.

Today, collaged, post modern culture has nearly reached the scale of totemization in some demographic sub-groups or tribes where every bush, small animal, mountain or river is associated with specific logos. This complexification of brands is nowhere more evident than on NASCAR stock cars with their sponsor names each carefully placed according to a rule-based hierarchy. Do Gibson and Stephenson see more than a visual sprawl on the hoods, fenders and doors, and would Picasso and Braque see the beauty in their surreal jumble of trademarks and logos?

The Old-New Soft Shell, or The Future is Taking Shape

In industrial design, things are oozing, melting and growing soft fast. Ovoid **"blobjects"** now recall the biomorphic fascination of the 1940s and 1950s. These are organic, natural shapes, but there is more at work here. These are the shapes of hardware that aspires to the condition of software. These are shapes that seek to be adaptable, customizable, approachable, cuddly — and even soft enough to account for individual accommodations. Seeking high-touch over high-tech, user friendliness becomes user obsequiousness: the new soft objects are so obedient they almost come up and lick your hand.

Soft shapes are dominant in cars such as the Ford Taurus, in innumerable video-game controllers and remote control units, and in furniture and computer equipment. Other cars such as the Hyundai Accent or Chrysler Neon seem more like cartoons than serious vehicles. More and more objects aspire to the playful quality of cartoon stars: from Ren and Stimpy to the Rug Rats to Putt Putt (the putty-soft, perky car of kids' computer games). On the computer screen, in the "Bugworld" area of the V-chat service on MSN, you find soft-bodied, amoeba-like-"avatars" — gesturing, on-screen cartoon personalities that seem to come from a Joan Miró painting.

In graphics, soft blurry edges dominate as well. The Neville Brody typeface called "blur," says designer Steve Heller, "is a kind of anti-Helvetica," subverting the modernist canon. Out-of-focus photographs hint at human failings, uncertainty, something only slowly coming clear. When pictures download from the World Wide Web, they generally do so in stages — sketchy and thin at first, filling in detail as more and more information arrives. The image on the Web browser is our new model of how the future will arrive.

These soft shapes and fuzzy images are a sign of a new attitude toward the future. As at least one recent ad puts it, "The future is taking shape," and it is a gentler, more speculative future, rounded-off like an economist's projection of an underground economy. These blobby shapes are like approximations of a future to which detail will be added later. The present is the youthful stage of the future: "the soft larval Now," as Vladimir Nabokov describes it in *Ada*.

These soft shapes evoke the streamlined shapes of planned futures — the shapes of the little cars that ran along Norman Bel Geddes's Magic Motorways at the GM Futurama in 1939, or, for that matter, the shapes of the fittings on the spaceship Enterprise. But they also serve to soften an often hard-edged technological vision of the future. Our ideas of how we get to the future have changed. The Darwinian model of evolution has been replaced by the ideas of complexity theory, of small changes that interact to create major new events. The imagery of complexity theory is that of the fractal — of **blobs of chaos** — and the new class of blobjects are like the genotype that will suggest, and are already suggesting, many varying specimens.

Frog has always been a hot house of ideas and the company's own magazine, *rana* (Latin for 'frog'), has provided a forum for debate and exciting imagery. Yet more is to be found on the company's own Web site (www.frogdesign.com) which not only promotes frog's philosophy, ideas and projects, but also acts as a test bed and demonstration area for new digital design experiment. 'Here was a great opportunity to redefine Web design,' says new media creative director Mark Rolston. 'Instead of building the site as a series of pages, we chose a different route and conceived the whole site as a unified experience, placing the emphasis on navigation, information architecture and usability. The centrepiece is the interactive timeline using Macromedia's Shockwave technology where, by using graphics and movies, visitors can explore the company's 30-year history.' This ever-changing site has attracted massive visitor numbers and a shelf full of awards, including a highly coveted Clio in 1998 – the first year an Internet design prize was awarded.

FROGDESIGN.COM
Web site, 1998

Following on the tradition established with *rana*, frog's Web site has proved to be a dazzling showcase for the company's work. Designers are encouraged to push the medium to its limits, experimenting with new formats, new site architecture and new ways of incorporating sound and moving images. Ideas tried and tested here also provide clients with a preview of the skills and ideas that can be incorporated into their own sites.

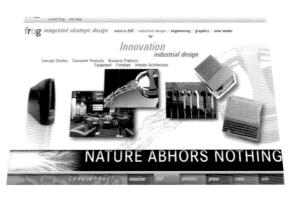

ONLY THE STRANGEST PEOPLE actually like going to the dentist, but since all of us should make regular visits it is good to know that check-ups and treatment can be made more comfortable and tolerable with some thoughtful design input. German manufacturer KaVo has been a frog client since 1971 and has during this time repositioned itself from being a middleground national player to an innovator on a global scale.

'A KaVo system offers superb physical and emotional human factors,' says Dan Harden. 'It even looks like it won't hurt.' Here, frog designers have been able to deploy the best in ergonomic design. The Estetica 1065 chair system, for example, allows the patient to lie back

in a comfortable, well-supported, fully reclined position. The chair is generously moulded to fit the body. The system is good news for dentists as well as patients: the instruments, on swivel arms, are all within easy reach and held within holster grips ready for use, and power cables are neatly managed. Colour has been cleverly deployed to reduce the 'fear factor': the chair base and central instrument platform are silver blue and dark red to reduce their apparent bulk, while the face of the chair and the instruments themselves are pale grey so that they appear to float above their supports. The chair unit is constructed in tough, enamel-coated metal and aluminium, and also uses injection-moulded plastic and polyurethane foam.

KAVO ESTETICA
1063/65
Dental unit, 1995

A balance of ergonomics and emotion, this all-in-one chair and instrument unit is conceived to alleviate the anxiety most patients feel when visiting the dentist. The sculpted seat provides maximum comfort but is also designed to allow the dentist to work quickly and efficiently.

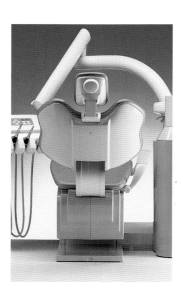

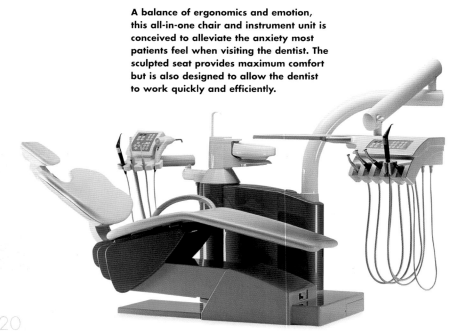

Apple and NeXt computers

THE RECEPTION LOBBY of frog's Californian office features a Zen-like area of neatly raked gravel – but in place of simple stones and boulders, there is an arrangement of computers. It's called the digital rock garden and here sit the dozen or so groundbreaking systems produced by frog's studio. At the back is the Apple IIC, the product which brought frog to the US in 1982. Apple visionary Steve Jobs had spotted frog's work for Wega and Sony and, wanting to make his mark on the emerging PC market, invited Esslinger to present some ideas for a new family of Apple products. Impressed by what he saw, Jobs offered frog a $2 million per year retainer to allow the company to set up in the US. Says Jobs: 'I wanted frog to be a resource for all of Apple; I didn't want people to worry about the meter running.' Frog went on to design the revolutionary Macintosh SE (launched in 1987), using the new Apple Mac operating system.

The Apple IIC was launched in 1984. A small, neat, beautifully crafted machine, with screen and drive encapsulated in the same pale grey housing, it stood apart in a market crowded with ugly, bulky, beige boxes.

APPLE IIC
Personal computer, 1984

The Apple IIC was instantly granted classic status: an example was acquired by the Whitney Museum in New York and *Time* magazine voted it Design of the Year.

APPLE MAC SE
Personal computer, 1987

Frog began collaborating with Apple in 1981 when it set to work on a radical new design strategy. The user-friendly Mac SE was one of the first products truly to reflect this new direction.

The appeal of the IIC and the Mac was instant and enduring, so much so that Apple's name became synonymous with user-friendliness, creating one of the most loyal customer bases in product history. 'With the Mac, frog introduced culture to technology,' says Dan Harden. 'In this mysterious and cold tech industry, along came an extraordinary product that was imbued with personality, beauty and simplicity. The Mac design, along with a great interface, finally broke down the barrier between machine and user, giving people the confidence to sit down and use a computer without hesitation. The Mac was more like your friend, instead of your slave.'

After leaving Apple, Steve Jobs set up NeXt Computer and launched a series of professional workstations which employed newly developed object-oriented software. Jobs wanted the appearance of his workstations to reflect the groundbreaking nature of his new system, and again commissioned frog to come up with a solution. The resulting design was elegant, sophisticated and, like Jobs' software innovations, somewhat ahead of its time.

NEXT
Computer workstation, 1987

Frog's innovative designs for NeXt included a stylish black monitor that appears to hover above the desktop. The computer itself is housed in a free-standing magnesium box, which further helps to eliminate clutter from the work space.

LOGITECH'S PRESIDENT Pierluigi Zappacosta paid frog one of its most treasured compliments when he saw his new company logo – the designers, he says, 'caught a glimpse of the heart of the company'. For Zappacosta, the design encapsulated the essence of Logitech. The solid green element represents the company's stability and positive approach; the eye expresses the company's vision and the user-friendliness of its products; the arrow is a computer cursor pointing skyward to convey forward-thinking and imagination; and the three radiating lines stand for dynamism, coordination and balance.

Logitech is a computer peripherals manufacturer which produces items such as pointing devices; with frog's help it has been responsible for nothing short of a reinvention of the computer mouse. (The company even produces a frog-designed mouse-shaped pointer for children.) Frog has worked on corporate identity and packaging, as well as the pointing devices themselves, and since its initial involvement has

LOGITECH
ICON
Company logo and
early designs, 1987/88

Full of impact but complex in its construction, this icon is graphic shorthand for a company that relies for its success on brilliant ideas, user-friendliness and dynamism.

seen Logitech rise to number one position in the computer peripherals market.

Among frog's most powerful designs for Logitech was the Palmball of 1994. In an era when the computer mouse was a stubborn, lumpen piece of plastic, this was a revolutionary design. 'The design objective was to create a stationary mouse that would be extremely comfortable to use and would reduce repetitive stress injuries, as well as being aesthetically appealing,' explains Dan Harden. 'The solution was a sculpted kidney-shaped form, with the trackball offset to meet the resting position of the index finger. Because of the hand's natural position, the top surface of the mouse slants down to the right for right-hand use. It also curves towards the front to accommodate the cupped palm and the natural curve of the fingers.' The result is a pointing device which is extremely comfortable to use, and also works well for users with limited hand and arm mobility.

LOGITECH MICE
Kidz Mouse and Palmball, 1994

It seems so obvious now, but it took a sense of humour combined with deadpan logic to produce the first mouse-shaped computer mouse (above). The Palmball (below) is ergonomically designed for maximum comfort with minimum effort.

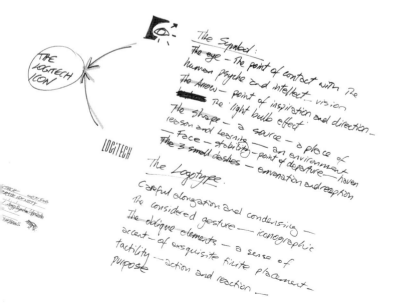

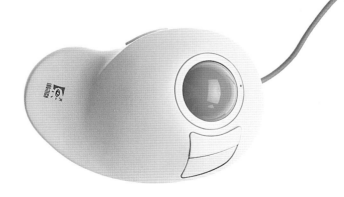

25

The Palmball was preceded by the equally innovative Trackman, which comes in both stationary and portable versions. The stationary mouse takes a sculpted nautilus form, with the trackball offset and lowered to meet the resting position of the thumb. The portable version is upright and can be used on a desktop or held in the hand. 'Here our goal was to create a three-button pointer, operated by the thumb, which would be small enough to be easily carried and used with a portable laptop computer,' explains Harden. 'We came up with an arch-shaped unit which accommodates the natural resting position of the hand.' Once again the ergonomic shape fits comfortably into the palm, while the large trackball and buttons give excellent precision and make the pointer easy to use. The Trackman can be easily adapted for right- or left-handed users and its casing is extremely sturdy so that it withstands travelling well.

LOGITECH
TRACKMAN
Computer input device, 1992

**The mouse reinvented as a snail...
the smooth shape of the stationary
Trackman fits snugly into the hand,
while the thumb-operated ball
gives the highest possible precision.**

LOGITECH
MOUSEMAN
PACK
Packaging, 1988–92

**Demonstrating the
power of its integrated
approach, frog
designed Logitech's
packaging to support
and complement its
work on products and
logos. The three line
elements from the main
logo reappear around
the product shot,
reinforcing the message
that the product is the
'star' of the pack.**

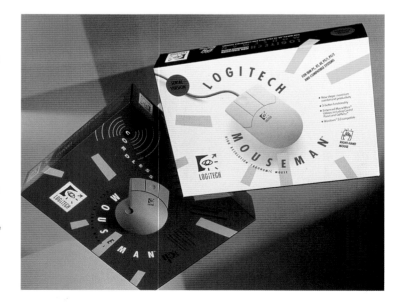

Logitech's shelf presence is unmistakable; unlike so much packaging, the boxes are bright, bold and eye-catching. The unified look provides excellent brand consistency.

27

HAVING IDENTIFIED the huge potential in the home computer market, Taiwanese manufacturer Acer decided to make a bid for its share of this booming area. At that time, in the mid-1990s, Acer was a relatively little known brand ranked tenth in the PC market. To achieve its aim, it sought out frog and came up with the brief 'to make the personal computer personal' – this was to be the first computer designed specifically for the home. 'They saw the potential for a new kind of product that would be somewhere between consumer electronics and a computer,' explains design team member Dan Harden. 'It had to be laden with easy-to-use features, and needed to fit the home and have a distinctive look.' The frog response was typically radical. 'We wanted to blur the boundary between software and hardware, and also to make people sit up and notice this new stuff. Too many computers offer the same performance and gadgets; we wanted to make the products really jump off the shelves. The client took a lot of convincing, but we got there.'

ACER ASPIRE
Home computer,
1995

The asymmetrical shape demanded the most advanced manufacturing techniques. Even the ventilation holes became part of the computer's distinctive look.

ACER ASPIRE
Home computer family,
1995

When the Aspire appeared on the market, consumers were in the habit of building their home computer systems from an assemblage of units by different manufacturers. With the Aspire they were drawn to buy the whole matching 'family'.

ACER
ASPIRE
Home computer
monitor, 1995

**The exquisite
detailing and
sculpted forms of
the Aspire proved
deeply attractive to
consumers looking
for a computer that
would look good in
the home.**

A frog team was assembled, comprising seven industrial designers and engineers. 'The overriding objective was to make a product for the home, one that would be relaxed, casual and simple. It had to look good next to jeans, sweats and pyjamas. It also had to appeal to the whole family,' recalls Harden. 'The home environment had a significant influence on the design – soft, rounded and complex asymmetrical sculptural forms were incorporated along with the rich, earthy colours of dark green and charcoal. We were picking up on domestic forms like sofas, easy chairs and cushions, and felt the dark, colours would look elegant and understated.' This was a radical departure from the conventional computers of the time. Even the ventilation panels received the design treatment, with a random pattern reinforcing the computer's offbeat personality. 'We gave all seven products in the Aspire range a harmonious, integrated look – they were seen as a family. This was good for Acer and good for the consumer – it meant that instead of shopping around for different components, people wanted to buy the whole matching set.'

Beauty here is more than skin deep, however. There's the thoughtful touch of making the system easy to set up through its incorporation of colour-coded cables which fit corresponding connectors. The tower and desktop CPUs feature easy-to-open cases which make upgrading the systems very simple, thereby extending their life. These clip-fit components have the added benefit of being easily recycled.

The eye-catching system, backed up by solid mechanical engineering, proved an instant success – Acer's post-launch sales in the fourth quarter of 1995 rocketed to $505 million, almost double those for the comparable period in 1994. 'The design work was really gutsy and has given the product a longevity which is unusual in this field,' says Harden. 'The Aspire range is still on sale and continues to look fresh more than three years later.'

ACER FUTURE
Keyboard, 1996

Designed for use with any computer, this keyboard has been developed using the latest ergonomic research. The board has been broken in half and angled to reduce wrist strain. In the centre it features a choice of cursor control, trackball or touchpad. Several keys have been relocated and a separate numerical keypad has been developed as a standalone unit.

Astralink ClipFone

DESCRIBED BY ONE MAGAZINE as 'the world's coolest cordless', this highly original domestic telephone system has a central station which can support up to four cordless phone handsets. It's all bright colours and science fiction shapes – very Star Trek in inspiration. When it was launched in the mid-1990s, the ClipFone immediately captured imaginations and became a must-have product. 'Eventually, communication products will completely merge with the body,' says designer Dan Harden. 'Until then, the ClipFone represents a step towards super-small, wearable devices. The ClipFone clips anywhere on your clothing and even back onto the charging base. Each member of the family can have their own uniquely coloured phone to use anywhere around the house. Your only tether is a radio wave.'

The phone unit brought together expertise from a number of frog departments. The trademark 'handfeel' quality has been achieved not only through appealing ergonomic shapes (a result of close collaboration between designers and model makers) but also in the selection of materials – a benefit of having in-house specialists. Many frog-designed products incorporate a subtle mixture of textured and smooth or hard and soft finishes. The technology tested the ingenuity of engineers – the phones can be used up to a range of 30 metres (100 feet) from the central set, and it is possible to transfer calls between handsets. Also, because space was at a premium in such a compact design, the engineers devised a way to make the clip function as both the power charge contact and the housing for the speaker.

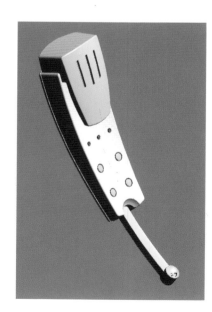

ASTRALINK CLIPFONE
Cordless telephone, 1996

Brightly coloured, lightweight and compact, this novel phone system was a truly innovative concept. Modern in its styling, it acknowledged the fact that all family members like to have access to the phone and would appreciate having their own handset. The system has a long range, allowing it to be used around the house and in the garden.

Sunbeam kitchen appliances

OCCASIONALLY THERE IS A DESIGN IDEA that's so logical, so sensible, that it makes you wonder why it was never thought of before. The Sunbeam toaster is just such an example. 'Our job was to take a mundane piece of houseware and to identify ways to improve such a familiar and standard object,' explains designer Sonja Schiefer. 'We had to ask ourselves, what would make it more useful, and what would make it stand out from the competition.' For Sunbeam the goal was to launch an innovative, improved-performance, up-market product that would boost the company's market share, which stood at four per cent in 1994. President of product development Dan Harden remarks: 'We saw a chance to renew the reputation of a manufacturer who once stood for innovation and technology, and who had helped to create the "appliance culture" of the 1950s with icons such as the beehive blender and the auto-pop chrome toaster, but whose products had since lost some of their strong identity. We wanted to bring back the feeling of optimism that characterized post-war America.'

The answer was to smarten up the case, improve performance and add a window so that you can see how your toast is cooking. 'It was such an obvious idea, and so right, and it cost just a few extra cents per item.' The brief also included the need to keep costs competitive – the launch price was to be around $34.99. This was achieved by reducing the number of parts and introducing snap-and-lock assembly, which saved on tooling and labour costs.

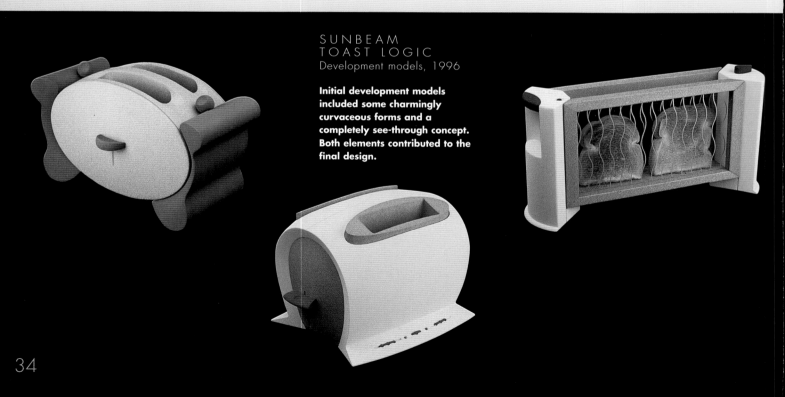

SUNBEAM
TOAST LOGIC
Development models, 1996

Initial development models included some charmingly curvaceous forms and a completely see-through concept. Both elements contributed to the final design.

The design went through an extensive model-making stage where the design team was given free rein to devise toasters in a variety of shapes and colours. Here frog's resident model makers played a crucial role in transforming 2-D sketches into 3-D objects. The lifelike prototypes received the final touches in the paintshop. The process moved along swiftly as frog engineers checked out what went on inside the case to ensure that the technology lived up to expectations. A microchip was developed to calibrate the heating elements so that the toast, or other food, would be cooked to the desired colour, taking into account such variables as internal toaster temperature and food density.

Cute, bulbous shapes were in favour for a while – the early designs adopted a strong and cheerful 'Good Morning' character. Then came a radical step with a completely transparent version in a rectangular box. Eventually the curves and transparency were incorporated into one design. The exaggerated, rounded forms were tamed to form the two narrow ends of the toaster, and a viewing window placed in the centre of the flat front. The window provides reassurance for the user that the toast is being cooked just the way they like it, and to add to the fun the toaster is sold in a choice of colours. Through the launch of this new appliance, Sunbeam has

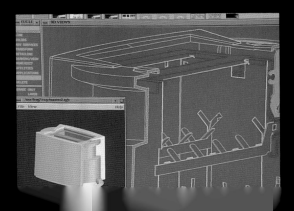

SUNBEAM
TOAST LOGIC
Design in progress, 1996

As with all frog products, the design is fine-tuned by the engineering department to ensure optimum functionality.

SUNBEAM
TOAST LOGIC
Toaster, 1996

The final product has a retro feel but also incorporates modern microchip technology to make sure the food is cooked to perfection.

made significant strides towards raising market share and has won a higher profile by selling the toaster through upmarket stores including Bloomingdales and Macy's.

Following the success of the toaster, frog's team was called in to work on further Sunbeam products. Pursuing the challenge to reinvent and improve, frog relished the opportunity to work on the new Osterizer blender in 1997. The result is an appliance that is bigger, easier to use, easier to clean and lighter than earlier models. In addition, performance was enhanced with a new blade (which handles a wider range of food types) and a clover-leaf shaped jar with three spouts which makes handling easier – whether you are right or left handed.

The Freshsource water filter, also launched in 1997, is an elegantly sculpted counter-top appliance. It is tall and slim so as to take up the smallest possible surface area. The device includes a powerful pump that forces water through a micro-fine filter to remove harmful particles; it then dispenses the water one glass at a time at the push of a button. The appliance is designed to be intuitive to use. Its whole shape is a celebration of water – the handle and spout are reminiscent of waterfalls, and the buttons are shaped like droplets.

SUNBEAM
OSTERIZER
Blender, 1997

A sturdy blender that delivers a whole batch of improvements over existing machines, the Osterizer features a high-performance blade and clover-leaf shaped jug to provide a positive grip.

SUNBEAM FRESHSOURCE
Water filter, 1997

The easy flowing lines of this water filter are designed to remind us of waterfalls, rivers, pools and droplets of water.

WHEN LUFTHANSA FIRST CAME to frog in 1995 it was seeking help in streamlining its check-in operations at Frankfurt Airport. After initial discussions, however, the airline agreed to explore the potential of adopting an integrated and strategic design approach to its operations, services and brand. 'We could see an opportunity to bring back the magic of flying, which is after all one of our most exciting and romantic inventions,' says Hartmut Esslinger. 'By combining the client's long and impressive history with a strategic vision of the future we saw there was a way of enhancing the brand and its level of service. We wanted to give passengers a smoother, more efficient and more enjoyable total experience.'

The process began when a team from Lufthansa landed at the Sunnyvale offices. 'At the start we had a good cerebral workout,' recalls Dan Harden. 'The Lufthansa team spent a lot of time with us, working through the company's brand architecture at the most seminal level, explaining the use of colours in the logo, the bird emblem, and the primary and secondary core values.' Lufthansa wanted the work to express not only its qualities of reliability, competence and perfection but also a new emphasis on friendly service and maximum comfort. Frog's task was to inject 'customer delight' into the flying experience, and create an optimistic, considerate and relaxed mood. 'People recognized that Lufthansa would be safety-conscious,

FRANKFURT
AIRPORT
Scale model of lounge
area, 1997

Any anxiety felt by passengers is smoothed away through the curved shapes and random seating patterns of the lounge areas. The designers' use of 'retro-futuristic' styling blends nostalgia with the latest technology; far from being functional holding areas, the lounges resemble the interior of a luxury cruise liner.

Passenger comfort is assured right at the start of the journey in the business class lounge, where the blend of glamour and luxury turns flying into a pleasurable adventure. The frog team studied the experiences of passengers and staff to identify where improvements could be made to the travelling and working environment.

FRANKFURT
AIRPORT
Ticket counters, 1996

When Lufthansa first contacted frog it was for help in streamlining the ticket sales and check-in procedure. From this initial project, frog has implemented a strategic and integrated redesign of the entire airline to improve its performance and levels of customer satisfaction.

FRANKFURT AIRPORT
Passenger tunnel, café and departure lounge, 1996

Every aspect of frog's design is conceived to enhance the excitement and romance of air travel. Shapes and motifs used in the interiors borrow from the language of aeroplanes, such as sweeping aerodynamic curves, wing sections, ellipses and cones.

honest, reliable, clean and on time,' says Hartmut Esslinger. 'We needed to add meaningful difference via the warmer, give-a-little-extra, emotional side of design.'

Frog's strategic approach involved getting back to the basic premises of air travel. 'In today's hypercompetitive market, even the most advanced technology is not enough,' says Esslinger. 'In re-examining the experience of flying, we rediscovered the importance of the airport as a place and as a space. We took a holistic and multi-disciplinary look at how the whole could be made greater than the sum of its parts. The ultimate goal was to create a sense of place and wellness for the Lufthansa passenger, to provide a positive experience from the ground level upwards.'

Soon after the early meetings, work began on streamlining the check-in desks and removing stress from the arrival procedures. Environmental improvements for customers were matched by those for staff. In collaboration with architect Michael McDonough, work then began on the whole Lufthansa terminal area at Frankfurt. Deploying technical engineers,

model makers and designers, frog produced a full mechanical design specification for the redesign of the gate areas and departure lounges. The best of the past – the airline's excellent reputation for safety and reliability, and the romance of early flight – was blended with the promise of improved performance in frog's retro-futuristic approach. The environment represents Lufthansa's new values through materials, colours and shapes, such as the curved metallic walls and counters which are reminiscent of aeroplane wings and other aeronautical forms. Business and first class lounges have been upgraded with luxurious seating areas, food and drinks bars, and conference rooms. The graphics team worked on the airport's characterful and highly legible signage. The overall impression is one of reliability and technical competence, mixed with friendliness and comfort.

In subsequent years frog has worked its way through the airline's different functions, redesigning aeroplane interiors, seating and even the in-flight cutlery. Its thoughtful observations and attention to detail have even included a water bottle holder in every seat.

LUFTHANSA
Business class seats,
1997–98

Since comfort during the flight is a major concern, especially to regular flyers, frog's team has developed new business and first class seating. One of the smartest features of this business class seat is the head rest, where the slide flaps can be adjusted to give some extra support.

Dual consumer electronics

BUILDING ON THE IDEA that there is no future without a past, frog helped reinvent the long-respected Dual consumer electronics brand. Their turbo-charged programme involved the design, production and launch of 22 products in just 27 months. 'The Dual name had been bought up by the German electronics chain store Karstadt. They came to us in 1995 wanting to invigorate the brand and launch a whole range of their own, from TVs and stereo systems to radios and CD players,' explains Greg Hom of frog's brand and strategy division. 'Dual was a famous name in the 1940s and 50s but had gradually been overtaken by competitors, so our task was to rediscover and reinvent the brand equity. Time was short and so the whole team moved at once.' Hom describes the process: 'Our early research was based around the idea of

DUAL ST
2110 VT
Stereo television,
1996

The elegant shapes are a celebration of the past – this could be the model of an old movie screen – but they also have an unmistakable air of modernity.

DUAL CCR 2010 R
Radio prototype and foam model,
1996

Frog's 'retro-futuristic' styling is perfect for the relaunched brand, which had been extremely well-known in the 1940s and 50s. Reminiscent of an old radiogram, the sculpted Art Deco shapes of the model are translated into the final prototype.

DUAL ST 2110 VT
Stereo television, 1996

**Sleek lines, elegant materials
and high production values
ensure that the Dual range sits
well in any interior. This
television is available in four
different colour combinations.**

"retro-futurism"; we looked back to the 1950s, the era of rock and roll and pop, fast cars with chrome fins, and emerging youth culture. After visits to museums, galleries and libraries, we amassed a stack of material for our trend boards. These collages of images, words and phrases were to help identify the essence of the products – they powerfully evoked of the feel we wanted to recreate. From here, early drawings were produced. Our engineers worked on functionality, while materials specialists advised on casings, the graphics team worked on the Dual logo and packaging, and new media designers worked on the revolutionary user-interface control panel that allows remote operation of the equipment.' This breakthrough design features an innovative digital menu and allows the user to operate all of the Dual products from one hand-held unit.

DUAL PDP 7010
Portable CD player, 1996

Simplicity and clarity are key to all the designs. This neat CD player borrows from the past with a body that resembles a plain chrome hub cap.

DUAL
Packaging, 1996

Frog's 'retro-futuristic' approach extends to the packaging design, with a range of colourful boxes that seem just too good to throw away.

The surge of action produced by frog's integrated strategic approach soon resulted in working prototypes and sample packaging (also based on a 'retro-futuristic' theme) to set before the client. The response was extremely positive and the first of the new range of products were soon in production. The Dual range has gone on to attract healthy sales and scoop numerous awards. The distinctive Dual Stereo Television, which incorporates new technology for greater image clarity, has won particular acclaim, including a 1997 Design Distinction award from *ID* magazine. The fruitful collaboration between Dual and frog has continued; among the latest products to be developed is a highly innovative multimedia centre combining video player, music centre and wide-screen TV/computer with Internet and game-playing capabilities.

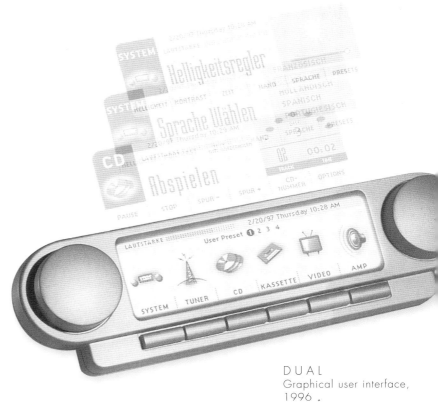

DUAL
Graphical user interface,
1996 .

The most advanced piece of design incorporated into the Dual electronics range is this remote-control panel, which eliminates the need for separate controls for TV, video and hi-fi. The user selects the product from an opening menu screen and then follows directions on the screen to switch on or off, raise or lower the volume and so on.

IT TAKES A COMBINATION of skill and well-honed intuition to design a product that goes on to become an integral part of a company's image – something achieved by frog with its digital storage tower for Trimm Technologies. This modular, hot-swappable enclosure for high-speed disk drives was designed using the latest CAD programs. Such programs, says frog's design vice-president Gadi Amit, 'allow us to be as flexible and creative as we want – the designer can become like a sculptor.' This sculptural quality is clearly evident in the Trimm tower's groundbreaking design.

In a world where there is generally little to choose between one storage tower and another, Trimm's product is distinguished by its 'flowing feature'. This subtle, smooth-formed trickle runs down the front of the tower to convey a sense of how the digital information flows through the interior of the unit. The feature ties all the drives together, and its distinctive image has since been used by Trimm in its advertising and as a backdrop to exhibitions and conferences.

TRIMM
TECHNOLOGIES
ULTRA TOWER
Digital information
storage tower, 1997

With so much computer hardware lacking any personality, this data storage tower is a real eye-catcher. The frog team has used a repeated organic-shaped motif to convey the idea of information flowing through the unit.

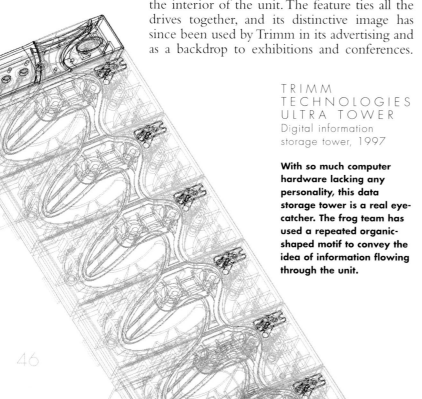

EMC CENTRIPLEX
Digital information
storage tower, 1995

With a design that plays on the idea of a tower, this information storage unit is conceived as a scaled-down piece of architecture, a solid and impregnable fortress that will protect any company's precious data records.

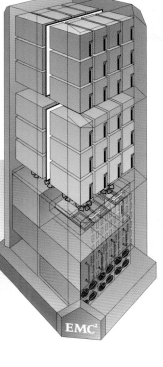

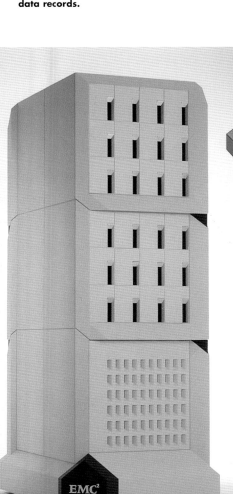

The design was conceived by frog to be intuitive to users, with a handle that is clear and easy to operate. In a further bid to distinguish the Trimm tower from its competitors, the face has been kept clean of ventilation patterns.

In another data storage system, this time for EMC, frog produced a wonderful architectural solution which plays with parallelogram geometry and references to Op Art. 'The infinite capacity of memory calls for an object which has infinite depth, but which is also as solid and strong-looking as possible,' says Amit. The EMC Centriplex storage tower employs the metaphor of an impenetrable vault; its appearance is that of a defensive structure, with a mesh of tight windows for the lower floors topped by a slightly more open structure above. The resulting tower has the aura of a most impressive skyscraper.

NO MATTER HOW daunting the technology, frog's ability to build in user-friendliness never fails to impress. Among its
recent triumphs is its work with global positioning systems. This equipment is used in a number
of specialist contexts, including land surveying
and the plotting of shipping movements. The
earth-based global positioning system communi-
cates with orbiting satellites and pinpoints loca-
tions to an accuracy of within 5mm (³⁄₁₆ inch).

When manufacturer Ashtech approached
frog it wanted to capitalize on the miniaturiza-
tion of electronic components and incorporate
into one hand-held unit a receiver, power sup-
ply, removable memory and radio link. 'Our
early research with professional mapping surveyors showed us that it's a lonely job out there,'
says design team member Josh Morenstein.
'Making this product a friendly companion,
with portability and tactile response, was the
least we could do.' Working with the experts
from Ashtech, frog's designers and engineers

accomplished their mission to make a single
integrated unit. The Z-Surveyor is shaped to fit
comfortably in the hand and, when used with a
carrying strap, it sits neatly with the shape of the
side of the body. The final flourish is in the fin-
ish of the casing, which has clearly borrowed
from the fashion and music industries and
resembles a Walkman or portable CD player.
Following the Z-Surveyor's launch in 1996,
Ashtech has become a new leader in the manu-
facture of global positioning devices.

Following on from this work came the
opportunity to work with Javad Positioning
Systems. When used with additional high-preci-
sion antennae this system can locate sites anywhere on the planet to within 1mm. Borrowing
imagery from space programmes and science
fiction, the elegant green and silver unit became
the first GPS system to combine a receiving
antenna, processing unit, batteries and a trans-
mitter. The highly distinctive colour was chosen
to make the unit easy to spot outdoors.

ASHTECH
Z-SURVEYOR
Global positioning
system, 1996

**Making complex
technology user-friendly
is one of frog's greatest
talents. This highly
sophisticated piece of
surveying hardware
borrows from the
language of nature, with
its topographical surfaces
and organic forms.**

JAVAD
POSITIONING
SYSTEMS
Global positioning
system, 1997

**They could be UFOs or
science fiction space
stations, but these neat
high-tech pieces of
equipment are used by
professional surveyors to
measure and chart the
earth's terrain.**

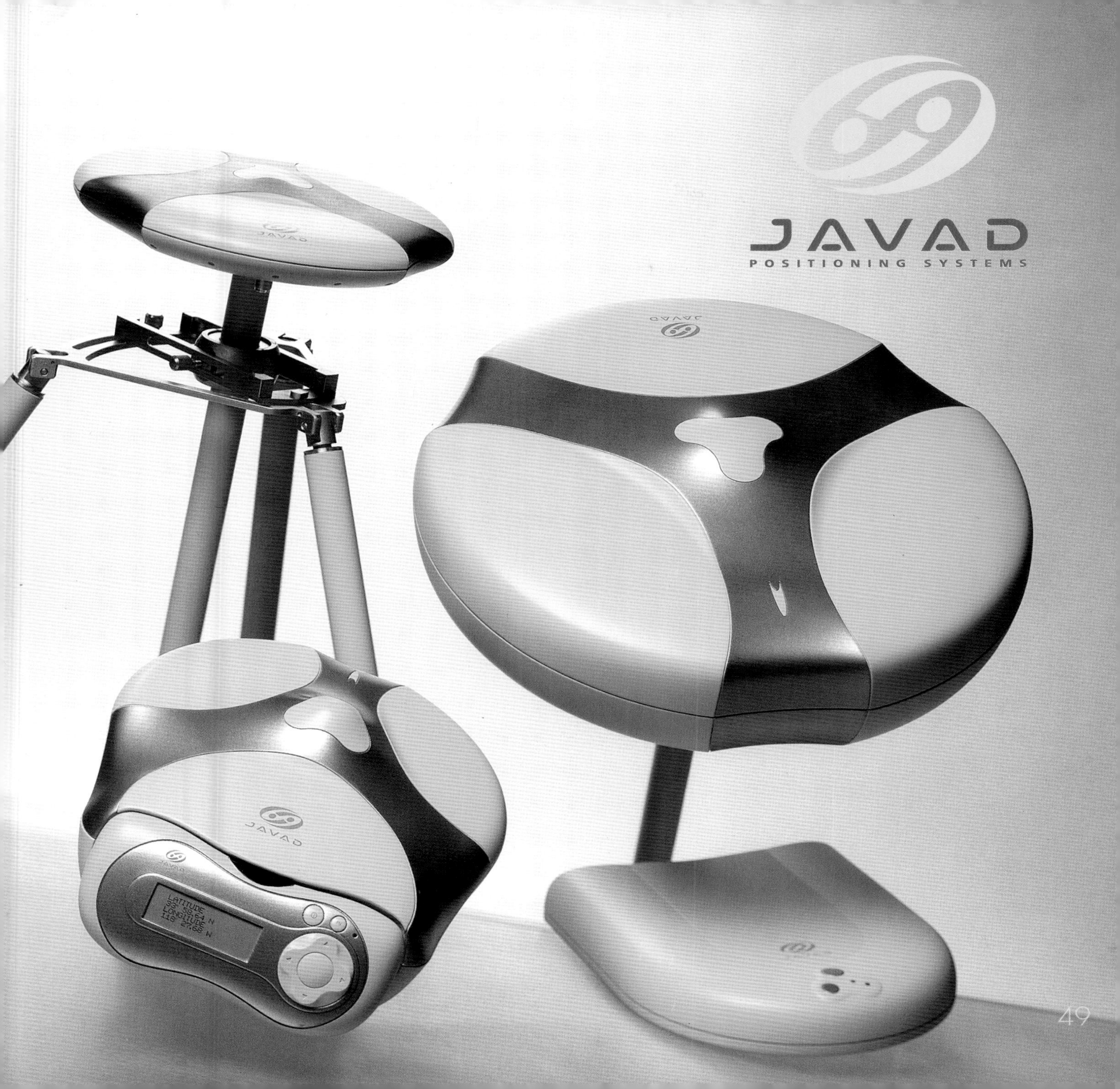
JAVAD
POSITIONING SYSTEMS
JAVAD
LATITUDE
33 59.64 N
LONGITUDE
118 27.68 N

WÜRTHNER T'BLADE
Ice hockey skate blade, 1996

Early computer-generated wireframe drawing and exploded view of designs for the revolutionary lightweight blade.

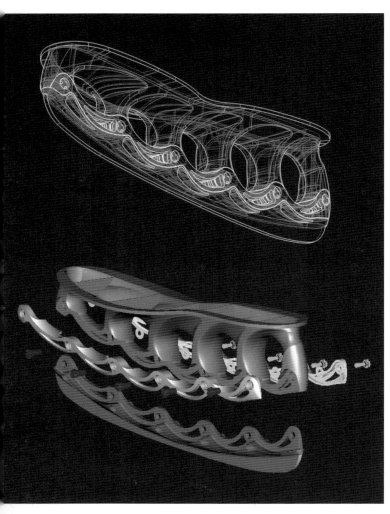

WHEN THE GERMAN-BASED sports equipment manufacturer Würthner approached frog to give its ice hockey skates an edge over the competition, little did it expect that it would be responsible for one of the most important and radical innovations in the sport for over a century. The client's goal was to solve a couple of age-old problems: it wanted to eliminate the need to resharpen skate blades (the grinding process results in jagged edges that inhibit performance), and also wished to reduce the weight of the skate blade, traditionally a large piece of hardened steel.

After the initial creative jam session, frog set its designers and engineers the challenge of making a skate that was faster and lighter than all others. 'We were going to put a huge hockey player on the thinnest strip of steel and expect them to travel faster than they ever dreamed,' says president of product development Dan Harden. From the first sketches, the design was transferred into the computer and tested for its strengths and stresses – the more material that could be pared away, the lighter and faster the finished skate. Using this process of elimination the team devised an elegant, minimal support structure which was composed of injection-moulded glass-filled nylon.

Alongside this work came the inspiration for a new type of blade – where the skate met the ice it would do so with a whisper of tungsten steel. This material met all the criteria – not only would it need no sharpening, but also it could simply be removed and replaced when worn. Moreover, because it is a conductive material set into a non-conductive plastic substrate the metal strip gets hot on impact with the ice and melts it; this helps the wearer travel faster. The resulting award-winning skate is a celebration of modern design, technology and materials – and is 25 per cent faster than its competitors.

WÜRTHNER
T'BLADE
Ice hockey skate
blade, 1996

**The completed skate
combines the skills of
frog's materials
experts with the flair
of innovative design.
It's light, it's fast and
it's cool.**

frog mobility

ONE OF FROG's most unusual and long-term projects goes under the title of frog mobility. This research unit, headed by Dan Sturges, has the task of finding new and sustainable methods of transportation. Sturges knows what he's talking about since he has designed and manufactured 700 of his own electric vehicles. But cars, he says, are only one part of the picture: 'The electric car would only solve our air pollution problems – we'd still have traffic jams. So we are also looking at changing attitudes, at making the electric car part of a new lifestyle where people become less attached to their vehicles. This also impacts on urban design – we are advancing proposals that will enable towns and cities to be less of a sprawl, places where people can walk to work or the shops or the café. Our models also make the most of digital technology. We don't need to go to the supermarket, for example; we could shop on the Web and then have the goods delivered to a neighbourhood collection point.'

In addition to these ideas and proposals the frog mobility unit is involved with major car manufacturers, colleges and urban designers, and plays a key role in drawing together research and ideas. Providing a model for experimentation is the Californian city of Davis, where frog is involved in a groundbreaking urban project to introduce electric vehicles on the city's roads. Davis is the home of the University of California's Institute of Transportation Studies, where Sturges works part-time as director of the electric vehicle project, EV Local. A recent development here is the introduction of neighbourhood electric vehicles (NEVs), which are used for short journeys. 'What makes Davis unique is the pre-planned neighbourhood centres, where no resident is more than two miles from shopping or schools,' explains Sturges. 'The aim is for Davis to become an EV systems city which will test all our ideas such as electronic shopping, car sharing and the latest electronic technology.

FROG
MOBILITY
PROJECT
Work in progress,
1998

As the western world's love affair with the internal combustion engine shows little sign of abating, designers at frog are working to find new ways of providing sustainable transportation and improving the quality of life in our towns and cities.

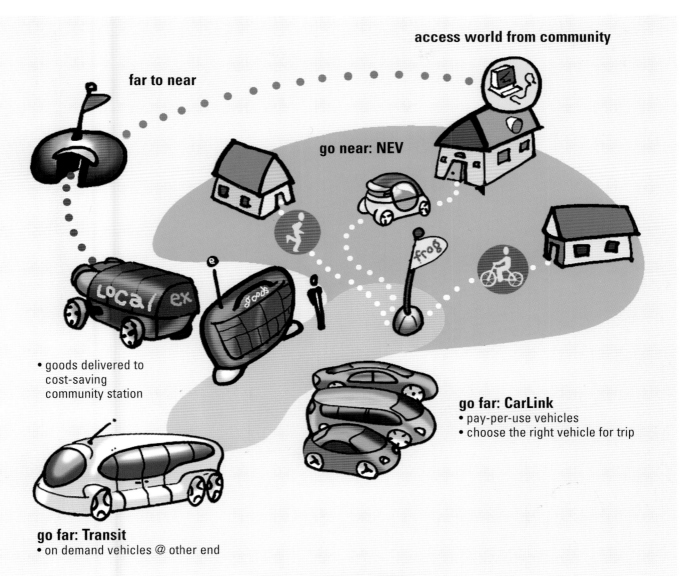

far to near

access world from community

go near: NEV

goods delivered to
cost-saving
community station

go far: CarLink
• pay-per-use vehicles
• choose the right vehicle for trip

go far: Transit
• on demand vehicles @ other end

frog mobility
improve life • intensify community

UNLIKE MANY TRADITIONAL design outfits frog has achieved impressive successes with its user-friendly digital media, which has included Web sites and remote control handsets. The skill has been in blurring the lines between software and hardware. 'Our heritage in the design of physical, tactile things has had a visible effect on the new media work,' explains Thor Muller, vice president of new media at frog's San Francisco office. 'Active consideration of things like kinaesthetics (the user's physical experience of interacting with digital interfaces), ergonomics, and the user's expectations of "tactility" are aspects of frog's new media work which set us apart from our contemporaries. The design process reinforces our belief that, despite initial appearances, digital experiences aren't disembodied from the physical world. The buttons, sliders and widgets on physical products like televisions and kitchen appliances can all be adapted for software user interfaces that meet similar functional needs.' Each project pushes at the edges of new media design and adds something fresh and surprising.

SAN FRANCISCO
MUSEUM OF
MODERN ART
Web site, 1998

Far from a gentle stroll round the collection, here surfers will discover a Web site that's provocative, engaging and interactive.

One of frog's most exciting sites has been constructed for the San Francisco Museum of Modern Art. Wanting a refreshing look for museums on the Web, the designers steered clear of the usual passive stroll round a collection and instead opted for a fully interactive experience. 'The notion of dialogue is promoted as soon as you enter the site. The first page prods users with shots of controversial art, and questions – such as 'Is this art?' – that invite the user to participate,' explains Muller. 'Like the museum itself, the site is always teeming with activity.

Key screens use movement to reflect the ever-changing landscape of the art world. Portions of the screen reconfigure themselves as the user watches – the pages never look the same twice.' Separate sections for particular exhibitions are built to reflect the work of the featured artist: a recent show on Keith Haring's graffiti art was shown on screen in a long subway tunnel, which visitors scrolled along horizontally.

The site for health products manufacturer GreenTree is devoted to shedding light on users' critical health issues, inviting visitors to ask

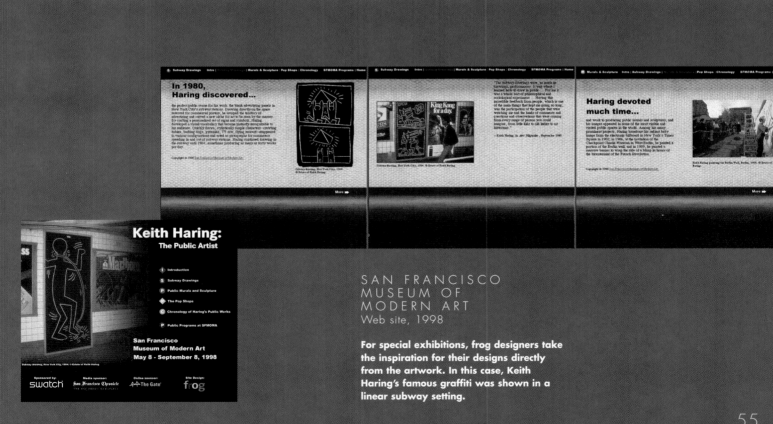

SAN FRANCISCO
MUSEUM OF
MODERN ART
Web site, 1998

For special exhibitions, frog designers take the inspiration for their designs directly from the artwork. In this case, Keith Haring's famous graffiti was shown in a linear subway setting.

Constructed as a health and well-being database and shop, this Web site is conceived to be easily accessible, especially to those who may not be familiar with the Internet. Visitors find their area of interest, which could be anything from athlete's foot to pregnancy, and then have the opportunity to buy the appropriate GreenTree products.

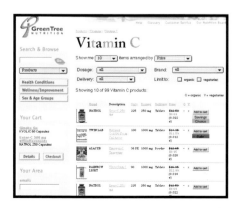

questions about their health and to understand their bodies better; there's also the option of buying goods online. Knowing that many of its visitors may well be new to Web technology, its creators conceived the site (which bills itself as 'the wellness center and superstore') as warm and welcoming. 'The ultimate aim, however, is to sell products and create return customers,' says Muller. 'Our design effort focused on creating a lifestyle brand, and building a site structure that used its deep levels of content to convert lookers into buyers.' Visitors search for the area that interests them – pregnancy, weight gain, the menopause or whatever – and are then directed to the appropriate information area and its suggested products. 'We have built in a "gravitational pull" that draws users from the opening page down to the buying decision page; we call this "sales momentum,"' Muller concludes.

The frog-designed site for the artist Enigma, who is signed to Virgin Records, serves as both standalone entertainment and promotional Web vehicle. It is highly stylized and cultish. Virgin asked frog to create a Web site that would promote Enigma while also invigorating interest among existing Enigma fans and attracting new listeners. 'Our response was to build a two-part site, comprising a promotional side and an enigmatic "world" that is a cross between a music video and a CD-ROM game,' says Muller. The site uses the distinctive album artwork as a starting point for its design, capturing the sensual, medieval tone of the music through a series of interactions. Multimedia technology (primarily Macromedia's Shockwave) was used to create an interactive musical underworld complete with medieval history, music, and even interactive chanting monks. Users solve a series of puzzles based on themes in Enigma's music. For the promotional section, frog displayed Enigma's music videos in Web-friendly formats and brought the printed song lyrics to life through

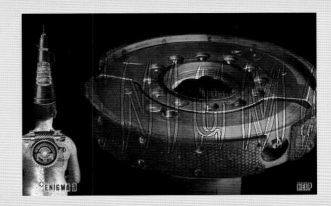

The complex and intriguing, myth-inspired imagery that had already been developed in Enigma's CD cases provided the designers with a rich source of material for the Web site.

These interactive demonstrations are used in product launches, promotional kits, trade shows and retail point-of-sale displays.

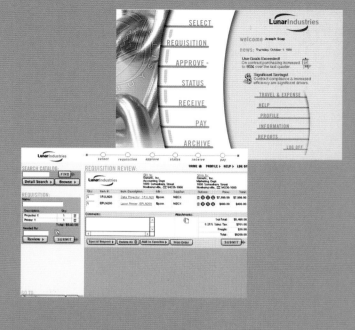

COMMERCE ONE
Software package, 1998

Large companies can streamline their ordering procedures – and thus increase cost-efficiency – via this package, which works over the office Intranet.

expressionistic animated typography. Bulletin boards were created to enable fans to chat with one another about Enigma's music and culture. The site has been critically acclaimed, winning numerous awards including *ID* magazine's Interactive Media Design Review, and the IPPA Award for Design Excellence.

On a rather different level is frog's work with Commerce One, whose software packages enable businesses to buy anything from a paperclip to a PC. The company has collaborated with frog on two main packages: BuySite, a purchasing system which works via the office

Intranet; and MarketSite, a Web-based catalogue of office goods from a large collection of manufacturers. 'The Web-based application is completely revolutionizing the way employees within large companies order the things they need to do their job,' explains Muller. 'Commerce One's software enables a company's Intranet to distribute the entire process of procuring supplies, materials and resources through a unified interface.' The result is drastically streamlined ordering and approval processes. The software uses colour as a navigational tool – in BuySite, for example, the blue zone is for search and browse,

A dream come true for anyone who has spent a lifetime looking for the perfect pair of jeans. Here you can combine Levi's expertise with creating your own bespoke design.

the grey is for selecting items and adding them to the shopping trolley, pink is the check-out and khaki enables buyers to track the progress of their orders.

Pushing interactivity to its limits is frog's work for Levi's, which has included a Web site and an innovative in-store design kiosk. The in-store service, called Personal Pair, enables customers to design and order a bespoke pair of jeans via an interactive screen. 'Our strategy was to pull customers into the kiosk experience through a cheeky, humorous interface that is in keeping with the style and aesthetic of Levi's,'

explains Muller. Using graphic symbols on screen, customers can choose leg shapes, stitching styles and materials to create their dream jeans. With every click of the mouse the picture on screen changes in response to the customer's choices. 'The user data is stored on a database where Levi's can access it, and where consumers can check on the status of their orders and change their profile information. These user profiles, which track preferences, tastes and buying histories, will ultimately allow Levi's to personalize its marketing approach for every user.' The kiosk won a silver Invision Award in 1998.

Chronology

1944
Hartmut Esslinger born in Beuren, Germany.

1966-70
Attends Fachhochschule für Gestaltung, Schwäbisch Gmünd, Germany.

1969
Founds Esslinger Design in Altensteig, Germany.

1971
Launch of the Hansgrohe shower head 'Tribel', which goes on to sell over 15 million units. Launch of the Wega 3000 hi-fi system. Esslinger begins working with Kaltenbach and Voight (KaVo), manufacturers of dental instruments and equipment (still a major frog client).

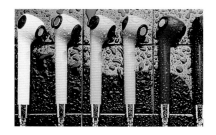

1974
Esslinger Design begins working with Sony. Begins back-page ad campaign on *form* magazine.

1976
Designs for Louis Vuitton (luggage and luxury goods) and Texas Instruments (electronics).

1978
Wega Concept 51K stereo admitted to MoMA, New York; Sony Trinitron is launched.

1981
Begins working with Steve Jobs of Apple Computer to design the Macintosh.

1982
Esslinger Design is renamed frogdesign. A second studio is opened in Campbell, California.

1984
Launch of Apple IIc; the computer is chosen for the collection of the Whitney Museum, New York, and is voted *Time* magazine's 'Design of the Year'.

1985
Frogdesign begins working with Logitech (computer peripherals). Conceptualizes new type of motorcycle sponsored by Yamaha. Begins bathrooms systems and ceramics for Villeroy & Boch.

1986
Frogdesign opens studio in Tokyo and resumes work with Sony, begins work with Olympus, Matsushita/Panasonic (consumer electronics), Epson (printers) and Sharp. Designs General Electric motor line.

1987
Launch of the Mac SE computer. Frox (multimedia systems) founded by Hartmut Esslinger. Work with NeXt Computer, Alessi (tableware) and Sun Microsystems (workstations).

1988
Exhibition 'FrogArt, 20 Years of frogdesign' is held in Philadelphia. Establishes office in Taiwan and begins work for Giant bicycles. Tableware designs for Rosenthal.

1989
Starts work for AT&T (answering machines), Melitta (coffee makers), nCube (Supercomputers) and 3M (office accessories).

1990
Works with Zeiss (binoculars), and Hyundai (workstations); frogdesign is cover story in *BusinessWeek* magazine.

1991
Moves Asian headquarters from Tokyo to Singapore. Works with Motorola (communications) and IBM (PC strategy).

1992
Frogdesign California institutes 'Integrated Strategic Design' (ISD), incorporating identity, engineering and graphics. Employs ISD on Zenith Data Systems (computers).

1993
Begins working with Packard Bell (multimedia PCs) to create brand and product line which instantly becomes a bestseller. Frogdesign is chosen 'Design Team of the Year 1993' by the Design Centre, Essen.

1994
Launch of world's best-selling microscope, the Olympus BX-40. Frogdesign California moves to new office in Sunnyvale. Begins to work with Disney. Launch of *rana*, frog's integrated strategic design magazine.

1995
Launch of Acer Aspire and Siemens/Nixdorf computers. Brand and product development for Dual consumer electronics. Begins working with Lufthansa on large-scale design strategy to include airport and aeroplane environments.

1996
Opens New Media division in Austin, Texas. Begins new media design for Compaq, Citibank and Conoco. Commissioned by *Macworld* magazine to design a prototype 'Mac of the Future'. Launch of Astralink cordless telephone, 't'blade' ice hockey blade for Würthner, and Sunbeam 'Toast Logic with Window' toaster.

1997
Develops Network Computer concept with Oracle CEO Larry Ellison. Launch of Ashtech portable GPS system. Sunbeam blenders and water filter introduced. Frog acquires Web development company, Prophet Communications, and opens San Francisco office.

1998
New York office opens, headed by Tucker Viemeister. Introduction of new colourful corporate identity. Frog wins Clio Award for own Web site and takes six Invision New Media Awards.

1999
Frog celebrates 30-year anniversary. Düsseldorf office opens in the 'Neue Zollhof' Building designed by architect Frank Gehry.

Index

Acknowledgements

The publishers wish to thank the frog teams worldwide for their kind assistance with all aspects of this book.

Design credits
Frankfurt Airport: pages 38–40, designed in cooperation with Michael McDonough Architect PC, Lori Weitzner Design, Architektürburo Belzner + Partner and Timothy Stebbing.

Photographic credits
Amdahl: page 11, Amdahl main frame.
Rick English (photographs): page 12, *Macworld* prototype; page 33, ClipFone family.
Dave Hannum (illustration): page 47, EMC tower.
Dietmar Henneka (photographs): page 8, Trinitron television and AT&T answering machine; page 9, 'Tribel' shower; page 22, Apple IIC and Mac SE; page 23, NeXt computers; page 24, Logitech mouse; page 25, Logitech mice; page 26, Logitech Trackman; page 28, Acer computer family.
KaVo: page 20, KaVo dental unit.

All photographs and images courtesy of frog.

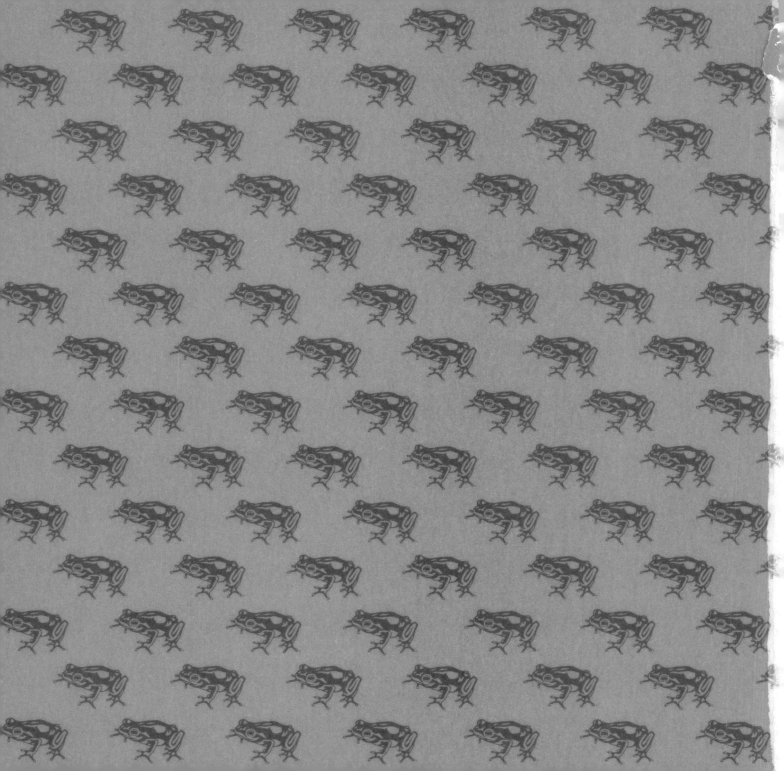